THE UNIVERSE *ROCKS!*

STARS AND THE DUST FROM SPACE

RAMAN PRINJA

QEB Publishing

To Kamini, Vikas and Sachin

Editorial and Design: Windmill Books Ltd.
Illustrator (activities): Geraint Ford/The Art Agency

Copyright © QEB Publishing 2012

First published in the United States in 2012 by
QEB Publishing, Inc.
3 Wrigley, Suite A
Irvine, CA 92618

www.qed-publishing.co.uk

A CIP record for this book is available from the Library of Congress.

ISBN 978 1 60992 247 4

Printed in China

Picture credits (t=top, b=bottom, l=left, c=center, fc=front cover)
Front Cover: NASA: APOD. NASA: 5r, 12-13, 18bl, 25br, 16-17; GSC 22bl, GRIN 2-3,
18-19, 24-25, 32; Hubble Site 4-5, 9, 12bl, 23br, 25t, 28-29, 30-31, 17tr, 24t; JPL 10-11,
14-15; NOAO: 22-23; Science Photolibrary: Richard Bizley 7tr, Chris Butler 6-7, John
Chumack 24bl, Lynette Cook 11t Eckhard Stawik 4bl; Shutterstock: 13tr, 26, 27b,
Andrea Danti 16l, Dan Lonut Popescu 27bl, R Valentina 27tc, 27tr, Guido Brola 21
*We have made every attempt to contact the copyright holder. If anyone has any
information please contact smortimer@windmillbooks.co.uk*

Website information is correct at time of going to press. However, the publishers
cannot accept liability for any information or links found on any Internet sites,
including third-party websites.

In preparation of this book, all due care has been exercised with regard to the
activities and advice depicted. The publishers regret that they can accept no
liability for any loss or injury sustained.

Words in **bold** are explained in the glossary on page 31

What Is a Light-year?

Distances in space are measured in light-years.
A light-year is the distance that light travels in one year.
- In one second light travels 186,000 miles
  (300,000 kilometers) or seven times around Earth.
- In one minute light travels 11 million miles (18 million
  kilometers) or to the Moon and back 50 times.
- In one year light travels 5,600 billion miles (9,000
  billion kilometers) or one light-year.

CONTENTS

Jewel Box of Stars

The night sky is a beautiful sight. Its stars sparkle and glitter like diamonds in a box of jewels.

In this book you will learn all about the stars. Are all stars the same? What are they made of? What type of star is the Sun? Will the stars shine forever, or will they burn out and die? Discover amazing answers to these questions and many more in this book.

Blue and Red Stars

Stars don't all have the same color. They can be blue, red, orange, or yellow. Stars have different colors because their surfaces have different temperatures. Blue stars are the hottest and red stars are coolest.

Betelgeuse and Rigel are stars in the **constellation** Orion. Betelgeuse is orange, and Rigel is blue. Rigel has a surface temperature of 68,000 degrees Fahrenheit (20,000 degrees Celsius)—that's three times hotter than Betelgeuse.

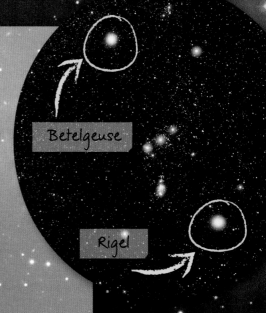
Betelgeuse

Rigel

Bright Ones and Faint Ones

Some stars are bright while others look faint. Stars can be brighter because they are more powerful. They put out more light energy, just like a giant floodlight in a sports stadium gives out much more light than a small flashlight. Some stars look dimmer because they are so far away.

The Giant Sun

Why does the Sun look so big? The Sun is the star in our **Solar System**. It appears as a very large light in the sky, but it is about the same size as most of the other stars you see at night. It looks bigger because it is much closer to us than other stars.

Light-years Away

Distances in space are unimaginably huge, so astronomers use a measurement called a **light-year**. One light-year is the distance that light travels in one year. Light moves very fast. It takes eight minutes to reach Earth from the Sun. However, it takes four years to arrive from our next nearest star— so scientists say that it is four light-years away. Rigel is 860 light-years from Earth.

Where Stars Are Born

One new star is born somewhere in our galaxy every year inside giant clouds of dust and gas.

The birthplace of a star is a **nebula**, a swirling cloud of **hydrogen** gas and specks of dust. Nebulae can have different shapes, and some glow with beautiful red, green, and blue colors.

Squeezed by Gravity

Gravity is the force that attracts one object to another. Inside a nebula gravity pulls the gas and dust together, squeezing it into a tight clump of matter. The clump gets hotter and hotter as the gas is pulled together. After millions of years, gravity has pressed the gas at the center, or **core**, so much that it is 59 million degrees Fahrenheit (15 million degrees Celsius). The clump is now a newborn star. It is a fierce ball of hot glowing gases.

The new star shines at the heart of a swirling cloud of gas and dust.

Making Planets

Unused gas and dust swirls around the new star, like a giant disk. It starts to clump into small rocks. These rocks crash together to make bigger and bigger bodies. They then trap gases around them, and finally we have planets with atmospheres, forming a solar system.

Rocks and planets form from the material left over when a star is born.

Star Shine

Gravity packs the hydrogen in the star's core very tightly. The hydrogen is in tiny units called **atoms**. Because the atoms are so hot they move around very fast and smash into each other. Several hydrogen atoms join—or fuse—together to make a new gas called **helium**. This process, called **nuclear fusion**, releases huge amounts of heat and light, making the star shine.

WHY TWINKLE, TWINKLE LITTLE STAR?

You've probably sung the famous rhyme about a star that twinkles at night, but have you ever wondered why stars twinkle?

You Will Need:

- Sheet of aluminum foil
- Large piece of cardboard
- Flashlight
- Scissors
- Glass bowl
- Water

TRY DOING THIS...

Here is a simple activity to help you find out what makes the stars twinkle.

1 Cut six little star shapes out of the aluminum foil. Stars about an inch (2.5 cm) across will do fine.

← 2 cm →

2 Place the stars on the cardboard so that they will all be covered by the glass bowl.

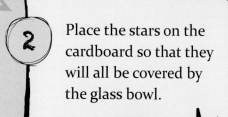

3 Fill about two thirds of the glass bowl with water and place it on top of the stars.

Bending Light

When we look at stars, their light travels through the Earth's atmosphere before reaching our eyes. Winds make the air in the atmosphere move around. The shifting air causes the light from the stars to bend.

4 Darken the room by drawing the drapes and turning off the lights. Shine the flashlight from the top of the bowl and look at the stars at the bottom.

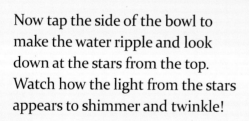

The light from stars twinkles as it passes through the Earth's atmosphere.

5 Now tap the side of the bowl to make the water ripple and look down at the stars from the top. Watch how the light from the stars appears to shimmer and twinkle!

...WHAT DID YOU LEARN?

The moving water in the bowl is making the light from the flashlight bend as it travels to the bottom and reflects back off the aluminum stars. The bent path followed by the light makes the stars appear to move, or twinkle.

LIFE-STORY OF THE SUN

The stars we see in the night sky will not shine forever. At some point all stars will run out of fuel.

Stars are born, they burn for a time, and then they die. The life cycle of a star takes **billions** of years. The Sun was born in a nebula about 5 billion years ago. Today, life on Earth thrives because of the warmth and light provided by the Sun. But things will be very different in our Solar System billions of years from now.

Big Fluffy Giant

The Sun's core has enough hydrogen to keep shining for another 5 billion years. Then it will swell up into a huge star called a **red giant**. After 100 million years as a red giant star, the Sun will then fall apart!

What Will Happen to Earth?

As a red giant, the Sun will be 200 times bigger and 3,000 times brighter than it is now. It will be so hot on our planet that the oceans will boil away. Even the rocky land will melt! But don't worry, this won't happen for another 5 billion years.

When the Sun becomes a red giant the Earth will be doomed!

Dying Sun

Earth

The Final Act

When the Sun has no fuel left its outer layers will be puffed out in giant shells called a **planetary nebula**. All that will be left behind will be the very hot and tightly packed core of the Sun, an object called a **white dwarf** star. The Sun will end its life as a white dwarf, gradually cooling over millions of years.

The Helix nebula forme...

REALLY MASSIVE STARS

There are incredibly powerful stars in the Universe that make our Sun look very small.

Our Sun has enough energy to shine for 10 billion years in total. Stars much heavier than the Sun shine more brightly. These massive stars use up their fuel supply of gases quicker than the Sun. A star that is born 20 times heavier than the Sun will shine 10,000 times brighter. But this star will only last for a few million years.

A doomed Massive Star expecting to explode in a supernova.

Making New Atoms

We know the Sun turns hydrogen into helium in its hot core (see page 7). But the centers of the biggest stars get much hotter, and the atoms are squeezed together to make atoms of heavier elements, such as carbon, oxygen, silicon, and even iron.

Rigel

The Sun

Big and Bigger

Some stars, such as Rigel, are so massive that they are born 50 or 100 times heavier than the Sun. The life story of a star depends on how heavy it was when it was first formed. Really massive stars have shorter and more violent lives than our Sun.

The Crab Nebula is the remains of a supernova. Chinese astronomers saw the explosion 1,000 years ago.

Giant Explosion

When the biggest stars run out of fuel they die in an explosion. As the huge star gets old, it swells into a supergiant star. Gravity then crushes the vast star into a core of iron. As it collapses, the massive star dies in a bright **supernova** explosion, which blows the outer layers into space.

SUPERNOVA BLAST WAVE

When a massive star dies in a supernova explosion, a shock wave blasts away almost all the gas layers of the star into space.

TRY DOING THIS...

In this activity we will use balls to explore how a blast wave can push out the layers of a star.

You Will Need:

* A table tennis ball
* A tennis ball
* A hard floor (not carpet or grass)

1 Hold the two balls together so that the table tennis ball is touching the top of the tennis ball. You can use two hands to do this.

1 m

2 Think of the smaller ball as the outer layers of a massive star and the tennis ball as the star's heavy iron core.

3 Hold the balls about 3 feet (around 1 m) above the hard surface. Now let both balls drop down at the same time so the tennis ball hits the ground first, with the table tennis ball falling just above it.

The shock wave of a supernova creates a huge cloud of hot gas and dust.

Precious Stuff

Many heavy chemical **elements**, such as gold and silver, are actually made in space during a supernova explosion. So someone wearing jewelery made of gold or silver is wearing a piece of a supernova!

4 When the tennis ball hits the ground, there's a little blast wave, but you can't see or feel it! Look at what happens to the small table tennis ball. It will bounce back up very high off the tennis ball.

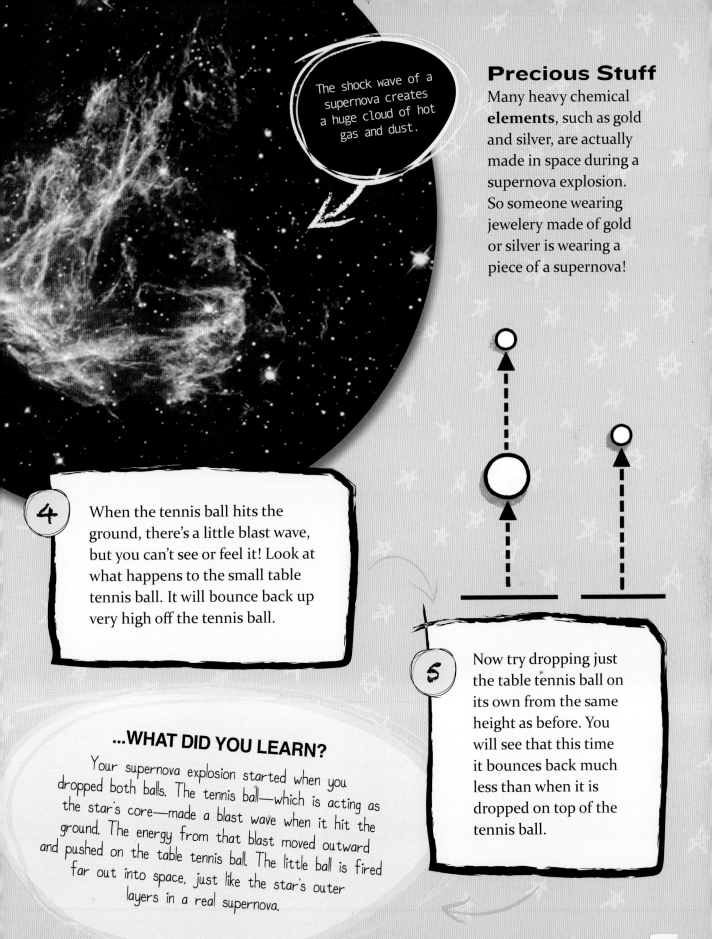

5 Now try dropping just the table tennis ball on its own from the same height as before. You will see that this time it bounces back much less than when it is dropped on top of the tennis ball.

...WHAT DID YOU LEARN?

Your supernova explosion started when you dropped both balls. The tennis ball—which is acting as the star's core—made a blast wave when it hit the ground. The energy from that blast moved outward and pushed on the table tennis ball. The little ball is fired far out into space, just like the star's outer layers in a real supernova.

ARE WE MADE OF STARDUST?

Scientists think there might be an amazing link between our lives on Earth and the stars.

Many chemical elements are needed to make up the human body. We breathe in oxygen and have carbon in our cells, calcium in our bones, and iron in the blood. Where did this stuff come from? Most scientists believe that the elements in our body were made inside stars!

Making the Stuff of Life

Scientists think that the **elements** needed for life are made by nuclear fusion inside stars. At the moment, the Sun is turning hydrogen into helium. As the Sun gets even hotter, the helium will be made into carbon. Massive stars can make many other elements.

A supernova blasts gas and dust into space, where it eventually forms a new star.

Making Planets

Chemical elements pushed into space from a dying star became part of the nebula that made our Solar System. The planets were made from the carbon, silicon, and iron dust that came from older stars far away. Maybe some of that stardust has ended up in us!

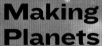

Stardust clumps together to form new matter.

Spreading the Elements

Thankfully for us the chemical elements that are made inside stars don't just stay locked in the stars forever. As a star gets older and runs out of energy, it starts to shed its outer layers of gas. When the Sun is a red giant star it will puff out lots of layers that have helium and carbon in them. In much heavier stars, the powerful supernova explosion pushes away the silicon, oxygen, and iron that was made inside the star and scatters it into space.

EXPLODING STARS

Dying stars make some of the biggest explosions in the Universe, and young stars experience raging storms.

During its life—and death—a star puts out huge amounts of energy. Sometimes this energy is released all at once in powerful explosions. Some explosions have so much energy that they can even be seen in other galaxies very far away from us. The bursts can even destroy the star itself. Let us take a closer look at the explosions made by stars.

The Earth could fit inside this bubble of gas blasting from the Sun 25 times over.

Bubbling Sun

Sometimes there are storms on the Sun. Super-hot bubbles explode from the surface making clouds of electrified gas. If a bubble hits Earth it can damage space satellites in orbit and even cause power failures on the surface. A giant solar storm caused a massive power failure in the USA and Canada in 1989.

Rocking the Universe

When stars 100 times heavier than the Sun die, they produce the most powerful explosions of all. Known as a **hypernova**, one of these incredible blasts packs more power than 10,000 normal supernovae put together! Hypernovae rock the Universe!

As the gas is blasted out from a supernova, it becomes hotter than the surface of the Sun..

Supernova

A supernova is one of the most powerful events in the Universe. We saw earlier how stars much heavier than the Sun end their lives in awesome blasts that rip them apart. The blast from a supernova will throw matter into space at an amazing speed of 25,000 miles (40,000 kilometers) per second. A supernova explosion is 10 billion times as bright as the Sun. It can even outshine the galaxy it is in.

COUNTING THE STARS

There are almost 200 billion stars in our Galaxy, but how many can you see with just your eyes?

TRY DOING THIS...

In this activity you can build a simple viewer to count how many stars are visible in the night sky. You can learn about why the night sky looks different when viewed from different locations.

You Will Need:

* Large piece of stiff cardboard 8 x 8 inches (20.3 x 20.3 cm)
* Ruler
* Pencil
* Scissors
* Long length of strong string
* Notebook

8 in (20 cm)

0.5 in (1.5 cm)

7 in (18 cm)

Light Pollution!

You should notice that the star counts made in dark locations, such as the countryside, are much higher than in a city. This is because light pollution from the streetlamps and buildings in cities makes it harder for us to see the stars.

1 First make your viewing frame. Use the ruler and pencil to draw a 0.5 in (1.5 cm) border along each side of the card. Cut along the border and remove the piece in the middle.

Ask an adult to help.

3 Put the string around your neck and hold the frame away from you until the string is fully stretched. This will make sure that the viewer is the same distance from your eyes each time you use it.

2 Make a hole in the middle of one border. Cut a length of string 31 in (80 cm) long, and loop it through the hole. Tie the ends of the string into a knot.

Ask an adult to help.

Where Are All the Rest?

From very dark places on clear nights you can see almost 2,000 stars. The other billions of stars in our Milky Way Galaxy are too faint and far away for us to see them directly. Astronomers use powerful telescopes to view, and study, many more stars.

Some stars are brighter than others, and you need to look carefully to see them all.

 4 Go outside on a clear night. Hold up the viewer and count how many stars you can see inside the frame. Do this five times, with the viewer pointed toward a different part of the sky. Write the numbers in your notebook.

5 Add up the five values that you wrote in your notebook and divide the total by five. That gives you the average number of stars you saw through your viewer.

...WHAT DID YOU LEARN?

The window in your frame is about 40 times smaller than the full stretch of the sky. Multiply your average number by 40 to get an estimate of the total number of stars we can see in the night sky. Try using your star viewer in different locations, such as the countryside and in a city.

GRAVEYARD OF STARS

When stars run out of energy and die, they leave behind a graveyard of very weird objects.

With no fuel left to keep the star shining, the force of gravity takes over and crushes what remains of the star. The type of object left in space will depend on how heavy the star was when it was first born. Here are three awesome types of dead star—**neutron stars, white dwarfs,** and **black holes**.

A black hole is invisible, but its surroundings glow brightly.

Neutron Stars

Stars that weigh 10 to 20 times more than the Sun end their lives as neutron stars. Neutron stars are made in supernova explosions. What was once a huge star is squeezed by gravity to a ball the size of a city. To make Earth as tightly packed as a neutron star it would have to be crushed to the size of a raindrop! Neutron stars can spin hundreds of times in a second.

Black Holes

The heaviest of stars make the strangest objects in space when they die. Stars that weigh more than 20 times the Sun become mysterious black holes. After a supernova nothing can stop gravity from crushing the matter that is left. When you make something smaller by crushing it, its gravity becomes even stronger. A black hole crams the star's material into a tiny space. Its gravity is so strong that even light cannot escape from it—that is why it is black.

White Dwarfs

At the end of its life, a lightweight star will be crushed inside its planetary nebula into an object called a white dwarf. A spoonful of white dwarf would weigh as much on Earth as an elephant!

23

RECYCLING IN SPACE

The life-story of a star keeps an amazing cosmic cycle turning as new stars form from dead ones.

Over billions of years chemical elements are recycled several times over. This process is very important in providing the material needed to make planets, oceans, and life. Let's go around the cosmic cycle.

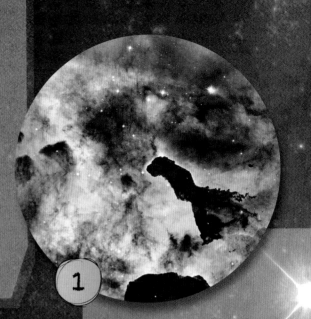

1

Clouds in Space

We start the cycle with the giant cloud of gas from which stars are made. Lots of hydrogen and other elements are found in these star-making factories.

The elements found on Earth are made inside stars.

2

Stars shine for billions of years.

Star Life

Once a star is born, it spends its life releasing the energy that makes it shine. The energy comes from nuclear fusion in its fiercely hot center. During fusion, hydrogen, helium, carbon, oxygen, iron, and other elements are made inside stars.

Spreading Stardust

The chemical elements made inside stars are released into space as the stars get older. Red giant stars and supernova explosions spew enormous amounts of stardust into space. These hot gases shoot into space and spread slowly over vast distances.

③

Red giant

④

Cat's eye Nebula

Back into the Clouds

After billions of years, the outer layers blasted out when a star dies will join other nebulae out in space. The clouds from several stars mix together until the stardust forms a new generation of stars. And the whole cosmic cycle begins again!

INVENT A CONSTELLATION

Constellations are imaginary patterns in the sky. They are made up of lines between the stars. It's like playing dot-to-dot with the night sky!

TRY DOING THIS...
In this activity you get to make up your own constellation and write a myth about it!

You Will Need:

* Large sheet of black cardstock or thick paper
* Packet of silver star stickers
* White crayon
* Ruler
* Pencil and notebook

1 Place the black paper on a flat surface.

2 With your eyes closed, stick 12 to 15 silver star stickers on the black paper. Try to spread out the stars a little as you place them—don't bunch them close together.

Constellations are a way of organizing the random pattern made by stars.

Sailing by the Stars

Constellations have had an important role in human history. They have been used by ancient civilizations to tell myths and stories. Sailors used constellations to navigate across the oceans. There are 88 constellations in the sky, including famous ones such as Orion (the Hunter), Scorpio (the Scorpion), Taurus (the Bull) and Cygnus (the Swan).

Scorpio

Taurus

3 Now open your eyes and look at the stars. Imagine being an ancient astronomer. Think of a pattern you could make with lines joining the stars. Perhaps you can make up an animal shape.

4 Once you've worked out a pattern, use the white crayon and ruler to draw straight lines between the stars. Stand back and look at your new constellation!

5 Now your constellation needs a name and a myth or story about it. When and where does your story take place? What type of beast or character is it? Perhaps it has special powers. Maybe there's a big battle with another constellation!

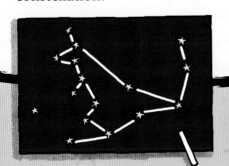

...WHAT DID YOU LEARN?

All constellations are just made up—even the ones used by astronomers. There are as many possible patterns in the sky as there are stars. The patterns people often see are everyday things, such as animals or people, but a constellation could be anything.

REALLY COOL STUFF ABOUT STARS

We've learned how stars form, how they shine brightly and then die. But there are many more things to discover.

What Are Sun Quakes?

Earthquakes on our planet are very dangerous. The Sun also has quakes, with huge ripples in the upper layers. Just like those on Earth, quakes on the Sun tell us about what the Sun is made of.

How Many Stars Are There in the Universe?

The best estimate is 20 thousand billion billion stars, or the number 2 followed by 22 zeros. That's almost as many stars as there are grains of dry sand on all the beaches on Earth!

Do Ghostly Particles Come From the Sun?

When nuclear fusion happens inside the Sun, some of the energy is put out as mysterious particles called neutrinos. These tiny particles can pass right through matter, just like ghosts! Almost a trillion neutrinos will pass through your body while you read this sentence!

Are There Diamonds in the Sky?

The insides of some dead stars are made of carbon, the same stuff that makes diamonds. The largest known diamond is inside a white dwarf star 50

Can Stars Crash?

Sometimes thousands of stars are tightly packed in a cluster. In the middle of these clusters stars can collide with enormous power. The wreckage that's left can be squeezed by gravity to make a new, much hotter star.

How Fast Does the Sun Move?

All stars in space are not still. Our Sun and its family of planets are flying at almost 44,000 miles (70,000 kilometers) per hour toward the constellation of Lyra. The Milky Way Galaxy is spinning, and the Sun makes a giant trip around it every 225 million years.

Where Do the Stars Go During the Day?

Only the Sun is visible by day. The rest of the stars are still there but you can't see them because the blue sky is so bright.

What Happens if I Fall Inside a Black Hole?

Your feet will feel a stronger pull of gravity than your head, so as you go into the black hole you will be stretched until you are as thin as spaghetti!

What Is the Largest Star in the Universe?

The largest of all known stars is called VY Canis Majoris. This monster is so big that if you placed it at the center of our Solar System, it would gobble up Mercury, Venus, Earth, Mars, and Jupiter!

Do Stars Shoot Water Jets?

When stars are forming they can shoot out jets of material. Sometimes these jets have hydrogen and oxygen atoms, which make super-hot water that shoots into space!

TOP TEN STAR FACTS

1. The brightest star in the night sky is Sirius.

2. The nearest star to the Sun is over four light-years away and is called Proxima Centauri.

3. The most magnetic star is a magnetar 1E 2259+586. It is more magnetic than 100-trillion fridge magnets!

4. The largest known star is VY Canis Majoris and it is 2,100 times larger than the Sun.

5. The fastest-spinning star is PSR J1748-2446ad. It spins 716 times every second.

6. The largest known star R136a1 has 265 times more mass than the Sun.

7. The hottest known star at 396,000 Fahrenheit (220,000 degrees Celsius) is a white dwarf called NGC 6302.

8. The most powerful known star LBV 1806-20 is 40 million times more powerful than the Sun.

9. The most distant supernova seen was 5 billion light-years away and is named ESO8802.

10. The fastest moving star is a neutron star known as RX J0822-4300. It is moving at more than 3 million miles (nearly 5 million kilometers) an hour.

WEBSITES

Hubble Space Telescope Gallery http://hubblesite.org/gallery

European Space Agency http://www.esa.int

BBC Space http://www.bbc.co.uk/science/space/

NASA http://www.nasa.gov/audience/forkids/kidsclub/flash/index.html

National Geographic Space http://science.nationalgeographic.com/science/space/

Online Star Map http://www.open2.net/science/finalfrontier/planisphere/planisphere_embedded.html

Astronomy Picture of the Day http://apod.nasa.gov/apod/

GLOSSARY

atom The smallest particle of any element.

billion The number equal to a 1,000 million.

black hole A region around a small but heavy object with gravity that is so strong that not even light can escape.

constellation An imaginary pattern drawn between different stars.

core The central part of an object, such as a planet or star.

element A pure chemical, such as hydrogen, oxygen, carbon, iron, or gold.

galaxy A collection of billions of stars held together by gravity.

gravity A force that attracts objects together.

helium A chemical element that is made inside stars when hydrogen atoms join together.

hydrogen A chemical element that is found inside stars. It is the smallest, lightest, and most common element in the Universe.

hypernova The most powerful explosion known in the Universe.

light-year The distance traveled by light in one year.

nebula Clouds of gas and dust in space. New stars are made here.

neutron star A very tightly packed dead star formed after a supernova.

nuclear fusion A process where small atoms are pushed together to make a heavier one releasing huge amounts of energy.

planetary nebula A cloud of gas seen surrounding stars the size of the Sun when they run out of energy and begin to die.

red giant A small star that has swollen to a much larger size than the Sun is today.

solar system Our Solar System is the Sun and the planets, moons, and other space objects that travel around it.

supernova A violent event that happens when massive stars explode.

universe All space, time, matter, and energy.

white dwarf A very hot and small object that forms when medium-sized stars like the Sun run out of energy and die.

INDEX